THE ULTIMATE GUIDE TO HUNTING™

INSIDER TIPS FOR HUNTING WATERFOWL

XINA M. UHL AND PHILIP WOLNY

rosen publishing's
rosen central®

New York

Published in 2019 by The Rosen Publishing Group, Inc.
29 East 21st Street, New York, NY 10010

Copyright © 2019 by The Rosen Publishing Group, Inc.

First Edition

Library of Congress Cataloging-in-Publication Data

Names: Uhl, Xina M., author | Wolny, Philip, author.
Title: Insider tips for hunting waterfowl / Xina M. Uhl and Philip Wolny.
Description: New York : Rosen Central, 2019. | Series: The ultimate guide to hunting | Includes bibliographical references and index. | Audience: Grades 5–8.
Identifiers: LCCN 2017048501 | ISBN 9781508181897 (library bound) | ISBN 9781508181903 (pbk.)
Subjects: LCSH: Waterfowl shooting—Juvenile literature.
Classification: LCC SK331 .U354 2018 | DDC 799.2/44—dc23
LC record available at https://lccn.loc.gov/2017048501

Manufactured in the United States of America

CONTENTS

INTRODUCTION

The U.S. Fish and Wildlife Service (FWS) estimates that there are over 110 million acres (44.5 million hectares) of wetlands in the continental United States. These wetlands include swamps, ponds, lakes, rivers, and ocean coastlines. They harbor critical habitats for wildlife, fish, and plants. North American wetlands also provide many recreational activities for the human population, including hunting duck, geese, and other waterfowl.

For many hunters, they are carrying on traditions that have been passed down along family lines for generations. Hunting provides people with experiences in nature, exercise, camaraderie, and meat untainted by hormones or antibiotics.

While hunting is a source of enjoyment and pride for many, it is not a sport to be undertaken lightly. It takes time and effort to learn proper hunting techniques and practice to be successful with those techniques. Confidence and knowledge is not developed immediately, and even hunters who have hunted waterfowl regularly learn new things every time they go out.

Hunting involves following local laws and regulations, not only for safety, but also to care for wilderness resources properly. Fees from hunting licenses support efforts to protect wetlands—efforts that are greatly needed. The decades between the 1950s and 1970s saw more than 500,000 acres (202,343 ha) of wetlands lost every year. While more than half of the nation's original wetlands were lost by the 1980s, during the last thirty years the loss of wetlands has slowed substantially. Dedicated conservationists, including hunters and outdoorsmen, have been part of this effort. It's more important than ever to carefully follow laws and regulations in order to safeguard this valuable resource for years to come.

Duck hunting can be an exciting rite of passage for many beginning hunters.

Hunting involves finding the proper habitat for your quarry. Waterfowl like ducks and geese can be found in fields near wetlands. There are four major waterfowl flyways in North America, covering most of the country. From east to west, these include the Atlantic, the Mississippi, the Central, and the Pacific Flyways.

By learning about the birds' behaviors, you can make the best use of your gear and other resources, like hunting dogs, blinds, or boats. The choice of weapon is critical, including selection of ammunition. To handle a weapon, you must get instruction and practice and remember to clean the tools. Recommended gear and supplies like duck calls are covered in the following pages. Spending time planning and thinking about problems that could arise before they begin is helpful, too. While there can be no substitute for having your feet on

Hunting waterfowl can be a lengthy affair and one that requires specific equipment, like the decoys and camouflage clothing shown here.

the ground in a hunt, having knowledge and a plan go a long way toward helping you succeed in bagging waterfowl.

After the hunt is accomplished, there are procedures that must be followed in order to ensure the game is safe to eat. Equipment and other supplies must be cleaned and serviced for use next time. Even if your hunt is unsuccessful, you can tweak your techniques for following hunts, working to conceal yourself better, scouting more thoroughly, using better calls, and shooting more accurately.

FUNDAMENTALS OF HUNTING

At first, it may seem as though all a hunter needs to do is to gather up his or her firearm and head out into the field to search for waterfowl. The reality is more complicated than that, though. Safety and skills training are imperative for a sport that can result in death or great bodily harm for yourself and other hunters.

One of the first things any waterfowl hunter needs to do is to learn how to shoot. Specifically, beginning hunters must learn how to safely and properly handle a shotgun, including how to care for and maintain it and use and store it legally. State and federal regulations differ over what gauges of weapon can be used in certain wildlife areas. But there are universal rules about how to behave in the wilderness when armed with a potentially lethal weapon. Most of these rules follow the dictates of simple common sense.

Some readers may already be familiar with guns and hunting. Still, even if they have hunted deer, turkey, or other game, they may be new to hunting waterfowl. Even seasoned pros need to review the basics occasionally, in order to stay sharp and focused and not inadvertently develop any bad habits. As a result, this chapter will hopefully prove useful to both beginners and those who have already gotten their feet wet, so to speak.

Duck calls, decoys, shotgun shells, and camouflage clothing are some of the waterfowl hunter's basic equipment.

SAFETY AND TRAINING

All fifty US states require that new hunters complete some kind of hunter safety course. In most places, such courses are provided free of charge and are funded by the state's fish and wildlife service.

Let's imagine that a young person in North Carolina wants to go hunting. The North Carolina Wildlife Resources Commission schedules a hunter education course several times a year in each county of the state. There is no minimum age for the course, which is taught by wildlife enforcement officers and skilled volunteers. In this class, students will learn about wildlife conservation, hunter responsibility and safety, firearms, identifying wildlife, first aid and survival, and other important other aspects of hunting. All first-time hunting license buyers must take the course.

Another example is provided by South Dakota, where a similar introductory hunting course is called HuntSAFE. It is offered for those between twelve and fifteen years of age, who earn a hunter safety certification card at the conclusion of the

Jeff Barnes, a recreational safety officer for the Iowa Department of Natural Resources, teaches a hunter education class.

class. Under federal guidelines, students take at least ten hours of instruction in handling firearms. They also learn hunting safety, ethics, and the proper relationship among hunters, wildlife, and conservation. They complete a written test and often do live-fire exercises under instructor supervision.

Once the course is passed, an adult must accompany anyone under sixteen to obtain a youth small game license and a

migratory bird certification. The fees for the license and certification are only a few dollars each. It is important to remember that rules and fees vary among the states. The following chapter will cover licenses and other certifications in greater detail.

THE EXPERTS

Young people new to waterfowl hunting usually have a parent, older sibling, or other adult, such as an uncle or friend of the family with whom they go out on hunts. There are many different rules all over North America dictating the minimum ages for hunting alone and hunting with an accompanying adult.

For obvious reasons, it is a bad idea for someone with very little experience to go shooting alone, regardless of age. Yet even young people who are expert marksmen still need the guidance and supervision of experienced adults. That's why rules in every state require that if a hunter is under a certain age, he or she must be accompanied by someone eighteen years or older.

Hunting waterfowl is often a family affair that is passed down through the generations.

Getting practice, instruction, advice, and guidance from an experienced adult before hitting the field is a great way to become comfortable with a shotgun. Going to a local shooting range or some other place where it is legal and safe to target shoot is also a great idea.

YOUTH HUNTS

Many states and waterfowl hunting organizations actively promote youth hunting so that the next generation preserves and passes on the traditions and rules of the sport. To do so, they promote youth waterfowl hunts on designated weekends during the hunting season. Such hunts may include a day of instruction on hunting and gun safety, the proper use of shotguns, bird identification, ecology, hunting tactics, and other outdoor training.

RIFLES AND SHOTGUNS

One of the first things a young hunter learns is that only shotguns are used in waterfowling. Rifles of any kind are illegal for this particular kind of hunting. Generally, a shotgun is fired from the user's shoulder. Unlike a rifle, which fires bullets, shotguns shoot small round projectiles, or pellets, called shot, or a single solid projectile called a slug.

Shotguns are usually smooth-bore weapons. This means the interior of the gun barrel is smooth, unlike rifles. The word "rifle" actually refers to the grooves—the rifles—in the barrel that help direct bullets with greater accuracy when fired.

At close range, shotguns are very powerful. Because shot spreads when fired, shotguns are effective against small and

BASIC FIREARM SAFETY

The Ten Commandments of Firearms Safety are an invaluable reminder of some basic common sense gun do's and don't's. Learn them and live them.

1. **Always keep the muzzle pointed in a safe direction.**
2. **Firearms should be unloaded when not actually in use.**
3. **Don't rely on your gun's safety.**
4. **Be sure of your target and what's beyond it.**
5. **Use proper ammunition.**
6. **If your gun fails to fire when the trigger is pulled, handle with care.**
7. **Always wear eye and ear protection when shooting.**
8. **Be sure the barrel is clear of obstructions before shooting.**
9. **Don't alter or modify your gun, and be sure to have it serviced regularly.**
10. **Learn the mechanical and handling characteristics of the firearm you are using.**

Source: Remington Arms Company, Inc.

moving targets—like waterfowl—because they don't require the hunter to aim with pinpoint accuracy. Shot becomes less effective and powerful at longer ranges. Shotguns are either semiautomatic or pump action.

CHOOSING GAUGES

When we talk about different types of shotguns, we generally refer to their gauge. Gauge refers to the diameter of the shotgun's bore and the shot used as ammunition. The smaller the gauge number, the larger the bore. The three gauge sizes most common in waterfowl hunting, from largest to smallest bore, are 10 gauge, 12 gauge, and 20 gauge. Each type of shotgun only uses shot appropriate to its gauge; a 12-gauge only takes 12-gauge shot, for example.

While the 10-gauge is the largest shotgun used for waterfowl and can kill ducks up to a 60-yard (55-meter) distance, it is also heavier and has greater recoil. Recoil is the amount of force pushing back on the hunter after taking a shot. As a result, the most common choice for waterfowling is a 12-gauge shotgun.

Shotguns are the weapon used by waterfowl hunters. They come in different gauges, which create different amounts of recoil.

For younger or inexperienced hunters, 20-gauge guns are often the best pick. Beginners should avoid guns with stronger recoil until they have developed their shooting skills and strength. Younger and less experienced gun users are often unprepared for the strength of the recoil, and the force of it can lead to injury and even shooting accidents.

LEAVE THE LEAD BEHIND

In the past, lead shot was commonly used by waterfowl hunters. However, it was eventually discovered that ducks and geese (among many other birds and other animal species) were ingesting leftover lead shot, mainly from lake and river bottoms. Lead poisoning is harmful not only to the animals, but also to those who dine on duck and goose meat.

As a result, all birdshot used in North American wetland areas must be nontoxic. Nonlead alternatives include steel, bismuth-tin, and mixed-metal shot using tungsten, nickel, and iron, among others. The cheapest alternative is steel, though many hunters note that because it is less dense than lead and other metals, it has a lower velocity and therefore a reduced effective range. Tungsten, bismuth, and other materials are as dense or denser than lead but are more expensive than steel. Shotgun manufacturers have worked on making higher muzzle velocities for their guns, with some success.

LAWS, RESPONSIBILITIES, AND MORE

S tate and federal hunting laws and hunters' ethics codes have been established in order to protect and preserve hunters' lives and well-being as well as the lives, health, and environment of waterfowl populations and their habitats. Care for the ecology of waterfowl regions is a responsibility that must be upheld by young and old alike to ensure that poor practices and abuses do not lead to the extermination of waterfowl and the loss of even more wetland habitats.

MAKING IT LEGAL

For new hunters, it may seem that there is a great deal of official paperwork involved before they can get out there and bag their first mallard. The good news is that many of these forms and applications can be filled out and submitted online. In addition, hunting licenses, stamps, and permits can be obtained in person at a variety of different locations: fish and wildlife offices, gun shops, the post office, and other certified locations. A hunter's best bet is to check with his or her state's fish and wildlife service, whether online or in person, to learn what paperwork must be completed and where it can be filled out and submitted.

After successfully completing a hunter safety course, most young people must be accompanied in the field by a properly licensed adult hunter (over the age of eighteen)—this means a parent, guardian, or other responsible adult. Rules vary by state, so hunters must be sure to familiarize themselves with the regulations and requirements of the area in which they will be hunting (whether in their home state or elsewhere).

In many places across the United States, young people can legally hunt waterfowl at an early age.

In Wyoming, for example, only those sixteen or older need a duck stamp to hunt waterfowl, but younger hunters must have a bird license if they are at least fourteen. Those younger than fourteen actually do not need any stamps or licenses, but they must have a hunter safety card, and their bag limit for waterfowl is included in the total limit for their adult guardian.

If a young hunter has her own license and stamp, she will also have her own bag limit. At the beginning of each hunting season, hunters should be sure to check for changes or updates to the state and federal hunting laws and regulations in place in their area.

WATERFOWL HABITAT

While individual state fish and wildlife services generally have oversight over the fish, game, and other wildlife within their borders, waterfowl jurisdiction works a bit differently. That's because waterfowl are migratory—that is, they migrate, or travel, to different areas during different seasons and easily cross borders. Since any given waterfowl population make their homes in two or more states throughout the year, the federal government has a responsibility for their well-being and the protection of their habitats. For this reason, the federal government demands certain things of waterfowl hunters over and above any particular state requirements.

FEDERAL CERTIFICATION

The Harvest Information Program (HIP) is a federal project in which hunters must participate. There is no fee for participating in the program, but waterfowl hunters complete a mandatory questionnaire in which they are asked to provide accurate information about the number and kind of birds they bagged the previous season.

The HIP can be filled out online or in person at any hunting license vendor. The HIP provides federal and state wildlife officials with valuable information. It aids them in estimating total bird harvests and setting dates for hunting seasons. The data collected by HIP also allows wildlife officials to better protect the health and abundance of waterfowl populations (and therefore the hunters' pastime) by insuring that overhunting does not occur and the number of various waterfowl species does not fall too low. Hunters are required to get HIP certification for each state in which they hunt.

MIGRATORY BIRD HUNTING STAMP

All waterfowl hunters are required to get a Federal Migratory Bird Hunting and Conservation Stamp, known as a duck stamp. This can be purchased at any US post office. All states also require a state duck stamp as well, available at any licensing agent. For convenience, some state licensing agents buy federal duck stamps to resell to hunters so that they can buy both required stamps at one time in one place. But it is not guaranteed that any given state licensing agent will have federal duck stamps on hand.

Hunters must also have a valid state hunting license. This is generally required for each state they plan to hunt in, if more than one. Some states will honor licenses from certain other states, but hunters can't assume this. They need to do the research and find out exactly what licenses and permits they will need to hunt legally in their chosen destination.

KNOWING YOUR SHOTS

As discussed earlier, rifles and handguns are prohibited in water-fowl hunting. Only shotguns may be used, and many areas restrict the size of the shotgun to no larger than a 10-gauge. The possession and use of Steel Size T and other shot larger than BBB are often prohibited. It is important for hunters to check both state and federal regulations on what kind of shot is legal in their home state or the state of their destination.

In some cases, certain shot may not be used against particular kinds of waterfowl. Yet these restrictions are sometimes lifted temporarily or permanently. The latest updated information on legal and permissible shot can usually be found online, by telephone, or in person at a state fish and wildlife office.

Hunting waterfowl can result in a large haul or nothing at all. Be prepared for either.

SPECIFIC RESTRICTIONS

The amount of any type of waterfowl that can be killed is restricted. Rules vary among states, and even among specific wetland areas within a state, on how many of a certain waterfowl species can be bagged during a specific period. This is known as a bag limit. There are daily and seasonal bag limits. There are also differing limits for how many females and males of a species may be shot.

These bag limits change from season to season and are usually set not long before the hunting season opens. Scientists, fish and wildlife officials, and hunters' groups all collect information regarding waterfowl populations and habitats in the months before the hunting season opens to help determine the proper daily and seasonal bag limits for each species and sex. Bag limits for each season are posted online and distributed in hard copy to service centers that cater to waterfowlers.

HAPPY HUNTING GROUNDS

Waterfowl hunting takes place in wetland areas where ducks, geese, and other birds stop during their seasonal migrations. There are millions of acres of federal land administered by the U.S. Fish and Wildlife Service (FWS) as national wildlife refuges. These refuges are generally open to the public for hunting. In addition, federally controlled Waterfowl Production Areas (WPA) are

known as specific waterfowling destinations. Locally, many state parks and forests are also open to hunting, including special Wildlife Management Areas (WMA). Individual counties in many states also own and operate public hunting lands.

Snow geese take wing from a lake at the Middle Creek Wildlife Management Area in Lancaster County, Pennsylvania.

However, much of the open land in many states is private property. In some cases, private logging and forest product companies own large parcels of territory but allow hunting. If they do not allow it, the land will be posted or marked with No Hunting and No Trespassing signs. Hunters must get permission—often in writing—from the landowners in order to hunt on private land. If the hunters are hunting on the land and are asked to leave, they must do so immediately. Trespassing laws are vital to the protection of human lives, livestock and wildlife, and property owners'

SPECIAL SEASONS

Waterfowl-hunting seasons occur when ducks, geese, and other game birds migrate away from cooling seasonal temperatures and toward feeding grounds in warmer climates—typically toward the end of summer and early autumn. Consequently, waterfowl-hunting seasons may begin anytime from September on.

A typical season may last anywhere from two weeks to two to three months, depending on the species of waterfowl involved and the size of their populations in particular states and regions. Permitted hunting of certain birds might even be broken up into a week or weekend at the beginning of autumn and another week later in the season. And different regions within a state may have different hunting seasons. For example, in the western part of New York State, the 2017 to 2018 season for ducks, coots, and mergansers was October 28 to December 6, and December 26 until January 14. However, these same breeds could only be hunted from October 7 to 29, and November 4 to December 10, in the northeast part of the state.

rights. Signs that say Keep Out, No Trespassing, or Hunting Prohibited are obvious indications that hunting or any other activity is not permitted on that land. Some signs may be posted that say Ask Permission/See Landowner. In this case, hunting privileges may be granted if the proper permission is sought.

HUNTING HOURS

Just as hunting seasons are restricted, so also are the times of day when waterfowl hunting is permitted. Most state and hunting areas have strict times when hunting may start in the morning and finish in the evenings. In some states, hunting starts at sunrise and ends at sunset. In others, people may hunt from a half hour before sunrise until an hour after sunset. Once again, specific hours for a state or region are available from game officials and on fish and wildlife websites.

PLANS AND SUPPLIES

Hunting provides escape from daily life in a pleasant, quiet, but wild environment. Modern-day life seems far away, and hunters find themselves tracking mallards through marshes, prairie potholes, or shallow pools.

Even though it's thrilling and peaceful to escape into the wilderness, hunters must understand the environment they are entering and recognize both its dangers and its fragility. Though it looks beautiful and feels serene, accidents can happen there that are potentially life threatening. And though the wilderness may appear pristine, the human presence within it can be destructive, so care must be taken to minimize one's impact.

It is important to know the environment and the waterfowl that are found there. Waterfowling is done in cold weather, sometimes in temperatures below freezing. Standing in icy water or hunting from a boat for long hours, waiting for an opportunity, requires patience. Ducks and other waterfowl are smart, have great vision, and can see colors. For these reasons, hunters have to rely on their wits, skill, and technique to bag them.

Ducks and geese often fly in a V shape. The shape allows for efficient energy use by the birds toward the back.

GETTING IN SHAPE

Much of a hunter's time and energy is spent waiting, trying to keep still and hidden. But hunters still need to be in relatively good shape for several reasons. Moving around in the wetland areas favored by waterfowl can be difficult and tiring, and a fair bit of physical effort is required to carry shotguns during an all-day hunt. Decoys, blinds, and other gear can also weigh hunters down. There is no guarantee that hunters will be able to drive to the exact site where they want to set up. On occasion, they might have to wade through deep water to get where they want to be or to retrieve birds they have killed (though waterfowl hunting dogs are often used for this purpose).

Performing some kind of physical activity daily and eating healthy will go a long way toward preparing a hunter for the rigors of the great outdoors. It's especially important to eat a good breakfast before going out in the field and to bring water

Hunters have erected these well-camouflaged blinds in order to hunt Canada geese.

and drink plenty of fluids. Packing trail mix or other high-energy, lightweight foods and snacks is also a good idea. These are useful not only for curbing hunger and thirst during a hunt. If a hunter gets lost or separated from the group, these fluids and snacks may save his or her life.

PREPARING FOR EMERGENCIES

In addition to guns and gear, a hunting party should always bring along a first aid kit while in the wilderness. Most waterfowling is done in relatively safe and accessible areas. Yet hunters in some areas will be out of communication with the outside world and possibly quite far from rescue or the nearest hospital. If an accident occurs, the person might not be able to move or be moved to get medical help. Even minor injuries benefit greatly from immediate, on-the-spot care.

Ready-made first aid kits can be purchased at sporting and hunting retailers and at drugstores. They can also be assembled at home. A good one will be waterproof and have disinfectant, first aid creams and ointments, different kinds of bandages, tweezers, and a first aid instruction booklet. Scissors or a hunting knife, disposable gloves, a flashlight, foil blankets, and numerous other items can also be added.

DIRTY AND DEADLY

In all the excitement of a hunt, it's often the small, unnoticed hazards that can be the most dangerous. In waterfowl habitats, like swamps and grain fields, there is always the chance of bits of debris (leaves, little twigs, gravel) getting into the shotgun barrel through the muzzle. Discharging a gun with even a small obstruction in it can be dangerous, even fatal. The barrel could rupture and harm the hunter and those near him or her.

If there is an obstruction of some kind in the barrel, it is a good idea for an experienced adult to remove the barrel and check it for blockages. One way is to carry a pull cord, cleaning cord, ramrod, or other tool to keep the barrel clear and unobstructed. Compact gun cleaning kits are also available in sporting good and hunting stores.

KEEPING COMFORTABLE AND HEALTHY

Waterfowl are often hunted when it's chilly, cold, or downright freezing, and the birds' habitats are always wet. A waterfowler's mission is to bag some birds while keeping relatively warm and dry.

Before going out, a hunter should be ready to invest in some weather-resistant and waterproof gear. It almost always pays to spend a little more on high-quality gear rather than cheaper goods that don't offer as much protection or durability. In some cases, quality gear can make the difference between a successful, safe, and enjoyable hunt and a physically uncomfortable or even dangerous excursion. Hunters who are not equipped with good gear may be forced to abandon the hunt if the weather changes suddenly or unexpectedly.

A hunter's clothing and antiweather gear should include a good pair of sturdy, waterproof boots. Good jackets, gloves, hats, caps, and pants go a long way, too. In addition to being waterproof, good outerwear should offer wind protection, too. Dressing in layers and bringing extra items of dry clothing are also a good hedge against the cold and damp and sudden shifts in weather.

Most experienced hunters recommend wearing wool or synthetic materials under foul-weather gear, rather than cotton. Cotton absorbs much more water when wet, and this moisture cools the body much faster in cold weather. Cotton is also more abrasive, irritating, and heavy when wet.

Hypothermia, a potentially deadly condition in which one's core body temperature drops too low for normal metabolism and bodily functions, can set in even at above-freezing temperatures. These days, well-designed synthetic clothing that is lightweight, comfortable, and quick drying is available for going afield. Bringing along a complete change of clothes just in case a hunter falls into water or otherwise gets drenched is also recommended.

HELPING YOUR HEARING

A waterfowler's ears are among his or her most important tools while hunting. Since hearing is also vitally important in everyday life, it is essential for hunters to protect their ears. Earplugs are a must to help avoid the permanent hearing loss that can occur as a result of firing guns.

FOOTGEAR

Waders are one of the must-have items for waterfowling. These are one-piece waterproof pants and boots worn over regular pants and shoes while standing in water or moving through wet and muddy terrain. There are two types: hip waders and chest-high waders. Chest-high waders are recommended for the greater coverage they offer, keeping hunters dry even when

Rubber waders can keep you dry and relatively warm while standing in frigid water for long periods of time.

they are crouching or sitting in water, very damp ground, or wet vegetation.

Waders are made from different kinds of synthetic material, such as neoprene, nylon, or Gore-Tex. In addition to keeping the wearer dry, good waders will have spacious, water-tight pockets that can hold shotgun shells, bird calls, and other items. As with other gear, it is best to spend a little more money on a good pair of waders that will keep a hunter dryer, warmer, and better insulated than a cheap pair will.

HIDE IN PLAIN SIGHT

Another must when hunting is camouflage. Ducks, in particular, see colors and have very good vision. They are also very perceptive and can often sense when something looks unusual or suspicious. Any hint of the presence of human beings makes them anxious and wary or scares them off entirely. That's why

CAMOUFLAGE

As Michael Hingle states in an article for *Wildfowl Magazine*,

> Over time, I've learned to match my camo pattern to each individual situation. For example, I'll never wear a dark pattern in a lighter colored environment or vice-versa. Similarly I would never think of using a snow pattern unless there was snow on the ground. In some situations, I'll wear the same camo pattern from head to toe, yet on other occasions I find it beneficial to mix and match various patterns.

> Hingle adds that he avoids camouflage with shiny buttons because they reflect light in a way that ducks find unnatural. A bigger mistake would be to hunt with fluorescent orange vests, which are used in some other types of game hunting. Fluorescent orange serves as a huge warning sign to ducks that humans are present.

a hunter's outerwear should blend easily into the surrounding environment. Hunters have a wide range of camouflage patterns from which to choose. Modern camo closely replicates the natural, irregular patterns of shading, light, and color found in field and stream.

CHAPTER FOUR

ON THE HUNT

While tips and tricks gathered from books and experienced hunters are valuable, the real test occurs when hunters go into the field and hunt themselves. There is a lot to learn about water safety, weather, decoys, calls, and blinds. Don't worry, though, there's also a lot of fun and adventure to be had.

STORMY TIMES

Learning about how weather affects waterfowl provides larger clues to their behavior, allowing for a more successful hunt. How do ducks react to weather, and how can hunters use this knowledge?

A storm front is good news for waterfowl hunters. Storms can mean harsher winds, rain, sleet, snow, and cloud cover. In these kinds of stormy conditions, ducks keep moving to find shelter. They then gather in these sheltered areas—like hillsides and lake coves—where they are easier to track. They also fly lower, where the winds are less powerful, which means they're at closer range.

Clouds also help duck hunters stay hidden. The sun does not reflect off the barrels of guns or other surfaces that reveal the presence of hunters. Even the light reflected off human faces can alert a bird to danger, and the shadows cast by hunters are also telltale signs of their presence.

When it's sunny, hunting conditions worsen. Ducks fly higher and are less restricted in their movements. They spot faces reflecting the sunlight and more easily notice the slightest movements and silhouettes. Just as hunters learn more and more

A number of well-disguised decoys have made this hunter's job easier, but hitting a flying target is not an easy thing to do.

about waterfowl behavior with experience over time, ducks, too, learn about the behavior of hunters. A few days of nice weather can help them better learn how to avoid getting bagged.

CONCEALING YOURSELF

Even well-disguised humans can stick out like a sore thumb. That's why hunters construct blinds out in the field to better hide themselves. A blind is any human-made structure that conceals hunters from their prey.

A natural blind can be constructed from elements gathered in the immediate environment, like sticks, leaves, and reeds. Some hunters even harvest their own wood before hitting the field, to "brush" their blinds. This saves them the trouble of finding brush where they hunt, which might not necessarily be available. Others even dig pits and camouflage them with things like corn stalks. They then crouch down in the pit to wait for duck or geese.

Some blinds are constructed of wood and are camouflaged, either with natural materials or with camo similar to that which hunters wear. People even build more complex, even luxurious, blinds, which have heating and other modern conveniences that protect hunters from foul weather.

BRINGING WATERFOWL TO YOU

Humans need to trick waterfowl into feeling safe enough to land nearby or gather within range. One important way to do this is with the help of decoys.

Decoys are realistic replicas of ducks and other waterfowl that hunters place in the water and other places where they want to attract live birds. For real birds, decoys create the illusion that

More than two thousand years ago, Native Americans west of the Colorado Plateau made duck decoys from reeds. Nowadays, duck decoys are often made of plastic and are quite lifelike.

other birds have gathered safely, away from humans and other predators. This makes them drop their guard and land nearby, within range of the hunters.

TYPES OF DECOYS

Decoys can be made from wood, cork, and other buoyant materials, but the most common and realistic ones are made from plastic. Plastic decoys have the added advantage of being widely available and affordable. In water, plastic line is used to connect decoys to each other and to the hunter. If a line is not used, the decoys will float away from each other and beyond the hunter's desired location. This would also make it very hard to collect and retrieve the decoys.

There are two main types of decoys: weighted-keel and water-keel. Water-keel decoys are hollow or made so that water will flow through them (though some are designed to fill up). Weighted-keel decoys are filled with sand and sealed, and thus are heavier, which is a disadvantage if a hunter is lugging around dozens of them. But, when tossed or placed in the water, they

SPREAD OUT

Every hunter has a different decoying technique, or several techniques depending on the birds involved, the weather, the location, and other circumstances. There's no rule of thumb, exactly. Different kinds of waterfowl respond differently, and this can change according to the environment, weather, and general "mood." Hunters watch how ducks respond to decoys and change the arrangements of them in response. A decoy arrangement is known as a spread or set.

For example, Michael Hingle tells _Wildfowl_ magazine that he gained insight into decoying through experience. Earlier, he had always set decoys too close together. He says, "It finally dawned on me that ducks and geese spread out when relaxed and move closer together when they become alarmed or nervous." By spreading his decoys out more loosely, in groups of four to seven, with 3 feet (0.9 meters) separating each decoy, Hingle attracted more birds. In addition, he also arranged a "landing zone" for incoming birds, making them more comfortable with landing, or "committing," in waterfowling language.

set, or right themselves, better. Their weight also makes them appear to swim more naturally, an important illusion for the fooling of real ducks. For these reasons, weighted-keel decoys are far more commonly used.

Water-keel decoys do have some advantages, however. They are lighter and more easily transported, meaning more decoys can be brought along. Newer models actually are better at setting themselves and remaining upright, and their "swimming" motions have become more lifelike. Also, because of their lower weight, water-keel decoys move more freely and naturally on days with light wind. Some hunters employ homemade methods to convert a water-keel decoy to a weighted-keel. Weighted straps, available for sale or fashioned at home, can be added as desired. These straps can be useful to keep decoys upright in various and changing wind conditions.

The decoys used by hunters should be matched to the birds being hunted. If resources are limited, however, and only a few decoys can be purchased or brought along, mallard decoys are the best bet since many waterfowl species respond well to them. With decoys, more is usually better, and a greater variety of decoys often works best in creating spreads that will make real birds commit.

WHISTLING WAYS

Another important tool in a hunter's arsenal is the duck or goose call. Calls are woodwind instruments, consisting of a barrel, a sounding board, and a reed. One uses a duck call to attract ducks to land or fly within shooting range. Waterfowl calls range in price from very cheap to quite expensive, but good ones can be found that are fairly inexpensive.

Different waterfowl species respond differently to calls at different times and under different conditions. For mallards, one of the most commonly hunted ducks, the call replicates the natural call of the hen (female). It should be sounded louder at a distance and quieter as the mallards close in. Mallard hens make the common "quacking" sound most people associate with ducks. Other waterfowl, such as pintail, teal, wood ducks, and the mallard drake (male), make a whistling sound.

Overcalling can make birds wary, but a well-placed response to a hen leading a flock can encourage the birds to commit. Keith McCutcheon advises readers of *Ducks Unlimited Magazine*, "Use your call sparingly. If more people approached it that way, it would be better on them, and on other hunters as well."

SPORTING DOGS

Hunters can go afield without one, but there's nothing like a good waterfowl dog to retrieve downed birds. A well-trained canine is a hunter's best friend, while an impatient, undisciplined, or disobedient one can scare ducks and geese away. However, one must always have patience, especially with a dog in training. Most of the dog's training should be done at home, not afield.

The benefits of bringing along a dog are many. Besides being natural swimmers, most bird dogs are very obedient and eager to please. A good one will keep quiet during the crucial moments of the hunt that require stealth. Dogs can withstand cold water and weather better than humans and are essential when retrieving birds in particularly dangerous conditions. With their keen sense of smell, dogs are expert at finding and retrieving birds.

There are several breeds of dogs that are common in waterfowling, chosen for their temperament, intelligence, and ease of training. Golden retrievers are among the most popular, as are

Dogs have helped humans hunt for thousands of years. It is likely one of the reasons they were domesticated in the first place.

cocker spaniels, springer spaniels, and Labrador retrievers. With a little bit of discipline and a lot of care, a dog can become an eager bird retriever and a loving and loyal pet for years to come.

WATERWAYS

Much waterfowl hunting is done from a boat. Only certain kinds of watercraft can be used for hunting, however. Rules vary among states, but water-fowlers can usually only shoot from rowboats and similar craft that are human propelled. That is, shooting from motor-driven craft or sailboats is sometimes restricted. In places where it is allowed, the motor must be shut off or the sail furled while shooting.

For waterfowling purposes, a boat requires concealment. Boat blinds are used, many times by using the natural terrain as cover. For example, using dense vegetation, whether on water or along shorelines to mask the boat's presence, goes a long way to fooling the birds overhead or swimming nearby. A boat blind may be brought along, or it may even be part of the construction of the boat itself. Boats allow hunters greater freedom of movement, getting them out on the water and into the sheltered places where waterfowl feed or otherwise gather.

Waterfowl hunters must be careful to be quiet. Loud engines on boats are usually restricted by local fish and game departments.

BEING SAFE ON THE WATER

The dangers of boat hunting include falling into the water and capsizing the boat itself. In cold conditions, this is especially dangerous because even with waterproof apparel, a hunter can develop hypothermia or drown due to being weighed down by the equipment and gear being carried and several layers of wet and increasingly heavy clothing.

Your boat should equipped with safety and emergency items, including:

- Life vests and a flotation/rescue device that can be thrown to someone who has fallen into the water
- Visual and sound-producing signal devices in case of emergency, like flares, whistles, and air horns
- A fire extinguisher
- A first aid kit
- Spare sets of dry and warm clothing

It is also absolutely necessary for the boat to have a water-proof container or compartment where these emergency and life-saving items can be safely stored, along with other gear.

CHAPTER FIVE

AFTER THE HARVEST

T he time has come. You've studied, researched, and read. You've obtained licenses and stamps, as well as necessary gear and equipment. You're ready to do what you've been working toward—bagging the ducks or geese.

THREE KINDS OF SHOOTING

There are three basic techniques for hunting waterfowl: jump shooting, pass shooting, and hunting over decoys. Jump shooting means sneaking into shotgun range of birds that are feeding or resting, often in small ponds, streams, or irrigation canals. When the birds discover a hunter's presence, they will start flying away, which is when a hunter should take his or her shot.

Pass shooting involves hunters taking positions in areas where they anticipate waterfowl to be flying by. This technique gets its best results on windier days, when birds fly low.

Hunting over decoys is perhaps the most widely practiced and classic way to bag waterfowl. Decoys are spread, the caller attracts the birds, and the cconcealed hunters wait in a blind.

Beginning hunters may be tempted to shoot at a target before taking the time they need for careful aiming.

TAKING YOUR TIME

All hunters have their own shooting styles and techniques. Beyond the essential rules of gun safety, there are several important guidelines to follow to help insure a more successful hunt and avoid common waterfowl shooting mistakes.

A common mistake is shooting too quickly in fear that birds will flare out of range. This often leads to errant shots and missing the targeted ducks and geese. Waiting just that extra two seconds after the birds have noticed the hunter leaves him or her with enough time to take a few shots before the waterfowl fly out of range. The shotgun should be mounted fluidly. Remember, this is not a quick-draw, fastest trigger finger contest.

FLOCKS AWAY

Another bit of advice is to aim for one bird at a time, rather than "flock shooting." Pick one bird and concentrate on it, rather than switching targets. As Wade Bourne notes in an article for *Ducks Unlimited Magazine*, "An incoming flight of ducks is 95 percent air," and a hunter is more likely to drop a bird by taking his or her time and aiming at only one member of the flock.

Beginning hunters might like to focus their attention on the closest, lowest, and easiest target. Aiming for a trailing bird, says Bourne, will put the hunter in position to try again with a second and third try as other birds in the flock flare up.

One or more harvested waterfowl can make a long, cold day of hunting well worth your while.

SPORTSMANSHIP

One of the reasons that skybusting is a bad practice relates to simple good sportsmanship. If the aim of waterfowl hunting was simply to bag as many birds as possible, then firing a machine gun from a tank would be acceptable. But shooting faraway targets

SKYBUSTING

Wade Bourne advises hunters to concentrate on the front of the target. On long, passing shots, most hunters will lead with their shotgun ahead of the bird. Those who don't will often take shots that pass behind the bird.

Using decoys creatively and intelligently can make a huge difference in getting off good shots. Typically, decoys should be placed no farther than 40 to 45 yards (37–41 meters). They should be set up in a shape that gives the birds a landing zone. Birds land into, and not away from, the wind, so the hunter should have the wind at his or her back. This way, the birds will approach the decoys from in front of the hunter.

Shooting at birds that are too far off—some call it skybusting—is a common mistake. An ideal range for most is 20 to 30 yards (18–27 m) . At that distance, a hunter can make out a duck's eyeballs clearly. If the bird's eyeballs cannot be seen, chances are it is still too far away and too early to take a shot.

with a shotgun increases the risk of merely crippling or otherwise injuring the birds, leading to a slow and painful death. There is no need to make a living creature suffer needlessly.

By the same token, other rules exist that ensure waterfowlers behave in a sportsmanlike manner. That's why, in many or all states, waterfowlers cannot:

- Hunt from a floating blind that is not anchored
- Use high-powered weaponry or explosives

- Use poison, drugs, or traps
- Chase birds on motor-conveyed vehicles
- Use electronic calling devices
- Use live, trapped birds as living decoys

Most hunters consider such techniques to be unsportsman-like or cruel.

STAYING SAFE

Always remember the Ten Commandments of Firearms Safety covered in chapter 1. Among other rules, hunters should always ensure that their shotgun safety is on at all times and only released when it is time to shoot. When loading the gun, keep the muzzle pointed up. In the blind, guns should be stored vertically and should not rest across a hunter's lap.

Hunters should always be mindful of their hunting partners when preparing to shoot. The hunting party should all agree ahead of time on each hunter's planned line of fire. If one hunter is shooting near someone else in a blind or elsewhere, he or she must be conscious of muzzle blast. Never shoot near or over a hunting partner. Stay in the blind during any shooting. When going out to retrieve a downed bird, a hunter should make sure to alert everyone and confirm that all other hunters have heard him or her and will hold their fire.

DRESS FOR SUCCESS

After a hunter bags a duck or a goose and his or her faithful dog has retrieved the bird from the reeds, what happens next? That all depends on what the hunters want to do with the bird. If they plan to eat the duck or goose, then they need to dress the bird, which means readying it for transport and consumption by removing certain parts.

It's important to keep the birds' bodies cool, so if the hunters have bagged several ducks or geese, they need to keep them separate and not stacked in a pile, for example. The birds should

When butchering a duck, it is helpful to know which parts of the bird are good for eating.

be laid out individually or hung up (in a blind, for instance) with duck straps.

Waterfowl are relatively easy to dress. It is generally done at home but may also be done in the field. First, the feathers on the bird's lower breast and abdomen need to be plucked. Using a knife, cut through the skin of its belly at the base of the breast area. Bend the bird backward and remove its entrails, or nonedible organs. Finally, pluck the remaining feathers and remove its feathery cape. The bird must be dried and kept cool, generally by putting it on ice in a cooler for transport.

To identify the bagged birds, all states require that the hunter either leaves the head or one wing, or both, on each bird brought in. In this way, gaming officials can ensure that hunters comply with bag limits on certain species and sexes.

For complete safety from contact with any possible germs or diseases, hunters need to wear latex gloves or some other protection while dressing birds in the field. While dressing a bird, a hunter should avoid eating, drinking, or other activities that might make him or her inadvertently touch his or her face. Keep the carcass and its fluids away from other food and drinks.

Finally, make sure to thoroughly clean and disinfect the tools used for dressing birds. While the contagious HPAI H5N1 flu virus—known as avian or bird flu—has not yet been detected in North American waterfowl, it is better to be safe than sorry.

When dressing a bird and preparing it for storage or a meal, several techniques can be used to remove its feathers. The bird can be plucked by hand or with the help of a mechanical plucking device. Soaking a carcass in near-scalding water a few times (without accidentally starting to cook it) makes feather removal much easier. Another method is to wax the bird. The bird can also be skinned or filleted.

TAG FIRST

One of the ways the authorities enforce bag limits is the requirement that each person tag his or her birds before either transporting them home or to a migratory bird preservation facility.

In North Carolina, for example, it is required that a bird—with either its head or one wing intact—be tagged with the hunter's signature, address, total number of birds tagged according to species and sex, and the dates of the kills. This includes any birds taken by the hunter or transferred to another person. Live or injured fowl that have been retrieved must be killed and included in a hunter's daily bag limit. If shipping birds, the outside of the shipment must have the names and addresses of both the sender and the recipient.

Now that you are prepared to get out there and take part in the popular sport and tradition of waterfowl hunting, remember to keep safe, abide by all the relevant rules and codes of ethics, and above all, have fun. Relatives, older siblings, family friends, and mentors will be happy to answer any questions or concerns that may arise and help provide safe, educational, and rewarding hunting experiences. So start getting ready for the coming season, and happy hunting!

GLOSSARY

afield Short for "going afield," referring to being in a waterfowl hunting area.

bag limit The daily and seasonal maximum limit allowed for killing specific numbers of particular waterfowl species.

blind The concealing shelter, made from various types of materials, in which hunters lie in wait for waterfowl.

bore The shaft or barrel of the shotgun through which shot travels and then exits through the muzzle.

call A woodwind tool that lets hunters mimic the sounds waterfowl make in order to attract them better.

commit In reference to waterfowl, to decide to land within firing range in response to calling and decoying.

decoy A realistic replica of a duck or other waterfowl used to attract birds to within shooting range; also can be used as a verb, as in "to decoy" a pond.

drake A male duck.

duck stamp Refers to one of the federal and state certifications that hunters must obtain to hunt during a particular season.

flyways The migratory routes, usually with easy access to wet areas, that waterfowl travel seasonally.

gauge Refers to the size of a shotgun's bore, which affects its shooting power.

Harvest Information Program (HIP) The obligatory and free federal certification program that aids the federal government in determining annual waterfowl harvest and populations.

hen A female duck.

skybusting Shooting birds that are too far away to effectively hit or kill.

smooth-bore Refers to a weapon in which the interior of the bore is smooth, contrasted with rifles, which are grooved, or rifled, within.

spread An arrangement of decoys; sometimes referred to as a set.

tagging The process of marking possession of birds by the hunter who bagged them; this is done to ensure proper compliance with bag limits.

waders Waterproof pants, often with attached boots, worn over the clothes, which protect the waterfowler from cold water and the elements in general.

waterfowl Migratory birds whose natural habitats are the wetlands and wet areas of the world.

water-keel Refers to decoys that are lighter than weighted-keel decoys and hollowed out so that water may flow through them.

Waterfowl Production Area (WPA) A federally set aside waterfowl hunting area.

weighted-keel Refers to decoys that are heavier than water-keel decoys and sealed and easier to keep set upright in the water.

FOR MORE INFORMATION

Canadian Wildlife Service (CWS)
Atlantic Region
Environment and Climate Change Canada
17 Waterfowl Lane
PO Box 6227
Sackville NB E4L 1G6
Canada
(800) 668-6767
Website: https://www.canada.ca/en/services/environment
    /wildlife-plants-species/migratory-birds.html
The CWS is the wildlife and hunting division of Environment
    Canada.

Delta Waterfowl
200-1555 St. James Street
Winnipeg, MB R3H 1B5
Canada
(877) 667-5656
Website: http://www.deltawaterfowl.org
Facebook: @DeltaFans
Twitter and Instagram: @DeltaWaterfowl
Delta Waterfowl is a major North American organization, based
    in Canada, whose mission is to secure the future of water-
    fowl and waterfowl hunting.

Ducks Unlimited
One Waterfowl Way
Memphis, TN 38120
(800) 45DUCKS
Website: http://www.ducks.org
Facebook and Twitter: @DucksUnlimited

Instagram: @ducksunlimitedinc
Ducks Unlimited, Inc., is a leading international organization that
    helps preserve wetlands, waterfowl, and the hunting tradition.

Ducks Unlimited Canada
PO Box 1160
Stonewall, MB R0C 2Z0
Canada
(800) 665-DUCK (3825)
Website: http://www.ducks.ca
Facebook and Instagram: @ducksunlimitedcanada
Twitter: @ducanada
The Canadian branch of Ducks Unlimited, Inc., conserves wetl-
    nands and other natural spaces for wildlife as well as people.

National Shooting Sports Foundation (NSSF)
Flintlock Ridge Office Center
11 Mile Hill Road
Newtown, CT 06470-2359
(203) 426-1320
Website: http://www.nssf.org
Facebook: @nssfcomm
Twitter: @NSSF
Instagram: @thenssf
The National Shooting Sports Foundation (NSSF) is the trade
    association for the shooting, hunting, and firearms industry.
    Formed in 1961, NSSF is a nonprofit organization that
    promotes, protects, and preserves hunting and the shoot-
    ing sports.

U.S. Fish & Wildlife Service (USFWS)
1849 C Street NW
Washington, DC 20240

(800) 344-9453
Facebook and Instagram: @usfws
Twitter: @USFWS
Website: http://www.fws.gov
The USFWS is the federal government's department in charge of
    conservation and game hunting, including waterfowl.

Waterfowl U.S.A.
National Headquarters
Box 500
Oak Forest, IL 60452
(803) 637-5767
Website: http://www.waterfowlusa.org
Facebook: @www.waterfowlusa.org
Waterfowl U.S.A. is a nonprofit organization promoting
    waterfowl conservation. It publishes *Waterfowl Magazine*
    for its members.

FOR FURTHER READING

Airhart, Tom, and Eddie Kent and Kent Raymer. *The Ultimate Guide to Waterfowl Hunting: Tips, Tactics, and Techniques for Ducks and Geese.* New York, NY: Skyhorse Publishing, 2017.

Bjorklund, Ruth. *Migratory and Resident Birds Explained.* New York, NY: Cavendish Square Publishing, 2017.

Carpenter, Tom. *Duck Hunting.* Minneapolis, MN: SportsZone, an imprint of Abdo Publishing, 2016.

Gaspar, Joe, and Jack Weaver. *Hunting.* New York, NY: Rosen Publishing, 2016.

Hemstock, Annie. *Hunting Laws and Safety.* New York, NY: Rosen Publishing, 2015.

Meyer, Susan. *Hunting Dogs: Different Breeds and Special Purposes.* New York, NY: Rosen Publishing, 2013.

Milner, Robert. *Absolutely Positively Gundog Training: Positive Training for Your Retriever Gundog.* CreateSpace, 2015.

Nickens, T. Edward. *The Best of the Total Outdoorsman: 501 Essential Tips and Tricks.* San Francisco, CA: Weldon Owen, 2017.

Shea, Therese. *What Is Animal Migration?* New York, NY: Britannica Educational Publishing, 2016.

Smith, Nick. *Waterfowl Hunting: Ducks and Geese of North America.* Minneapolis, MN: Cool Springs Press, 2014.

Wexo, John Bonnett, Paul A. Johnsgard, and Frank S. Todd. *Ducks, Goose, and Swans.* Peru, IL: Wildlife Education, 2014.

BIBLIOGRAPHY

Bibby, Marvin D. "Duck Hunting School Now in Session." *Game and Fish Magazine*. http://www.gameandfishmag.com /hunting/hunting_ducks-geese-hunting_gf_aa106602a.

Bourne, Wade. "10 Shooting Tips for Waterfowl." Ducks Unlimited. http://www.ducks.org/hunting/shooting-tips /10-shooting-tips-for-waterfowl.

Bourne, Wade. "Waterfowler's Notebook: Outfitting a Duck Boat." *Ducks Unlimited Magazine*, March/April 2010. http://www.ducks.org/hunting/waterfowl-hunting-tips /outfitting-a-duck-boat.

Everhart, Johnny. "Lessons in Waterfowling #1: Basic Fowl Language." Missourioutback.com. http://www.missourioutback .com/Stories/lesson1.html.

Everhart, Johnny. "Lessons in Waterfowling #2: Decoy Basics." Missourioutback.com. http://www.missourioutback.com /Stories/lesson2.html.

Hendricks, Bryan. "Finding Waterfowl Hotspots That Others Miss." *Game and Fish Magazine*, September 28, 2010. http://www.gameandfishmag.com/hunting/hunting_ducks -geese-hunting_gf_aa116403a.

Johnson, Julia. *Waterfowling: Beyond the Basics*. Mechanicsburg, PA: Stackpole Books, 2008.

McKee, Jennifer. "Wildlife Agency Takes Up Lead Ammo Ban This Week." *Billings Gazette*, February 8, 2010. http:// billingsgazette.com/news/state-and-regional/montana /article_7f364060-1513-11df-9e8f-001cc4c002e0.html.

Miller, Sarah Swan. *Waterfowl: From Swans to Screamers* (Animals in Order). London, England: Franklin Watts, 2000.

Office of the Secretary. "Five-Year Survey Shows Wetlands Losses are Slowing, Marking Conservation Gains and Need for Continued Investment in Habitat." U.S. Department of

the Interior, October 6, 2011. https://www.doi.gov/news
/pressreleases/Five-Year-Survey-Shows-Wetlands-Losses
-are-Slowing-Marking-Conservtion-Gains-and-Need-for
-Continued-Investment-in-Habitat.

Remington Rifle Company. "The Ten Commandments of Firearms Safety." https://www.remington.com/country/articles
/ten-commandments-firearms-safety.

Remington Rifle Company. "Waterfowl Shooting Tips."
https://www.remington.com/support/safety-center/safety
-and-shooting-tips/waterfowl-shooting.

Smith, Steve. *Hunting Ducks and Geese: Hard Facts, Good Bets,
and Serious Advice from a Duck Hunter You Can Trust.* Mechanicsburg, PA: Stackpole Books, 2003.

State of Minnesota Department of Natural Resources. "Hunting
Safety Tips." http://www.dnr.state.mn.us/hunting/tips/safety
.html.

Stuckey, Mike. "In Many States, Young Kids May Hunt Alone."
MSNBC, July 21, 2009. http://www.msnbc.msn.com
/id/31952727/ns/us_news-life.

Sutton, Keith. "Forecast Your Duck Hunting Success." Ducks
Unlimited. http://www.ducks.org/hunting/waterfowl
-hunting-tips/forecast-your-duck-hunting-success-weather
-matters.

Wexo, John Bonnett. *Ducks, Geese, & Swans* (Zoobooks Series).
Poway, CA: Wildlife Education, Ltd., 1998.

Yaich, Scott. "Crisis for America's Wetlands." Ducks Unlimited.
http://www.ducks.org/conservation/waterfowl-habitat
/crisis-for-americas-wetlands.

Young, Matt, ed. 161 *Waterfowling Secrets (by Ducks Unlimited
Magazine Staff)*. Memphis, TN: Ducks Unlimited, Inc., 2002.

INDEX

ABOUT THE AUTHORS

Xina M. Uhl has written numerous educational books for young people, in addition to textbooks, teacher's guides, lessons, and assessment questions. She has tackled subjects including sports, history, biographies, technology, and health concerns. Although she has friends and family who hunt, she shoots animals only through her camera lens. Her blog details her publications as well as interesting facts and the occasional cat picture.

Philip Wolny is a writer and editor living in New York. As a child, he spent a considerable amount of time in the company of duck hunters during vacations in Tennessee.

ABOUT THE CONSULTANT

Benjamin Cowan has over twenty years of both big game and small game hunting experience. In addition to being an avid hunter, Cowan is also a member of many conservation organizations. He currently resides in west Tennessee.

PHOTO CREDITS

Cover Monica Viora/Shutterstock.com; back cover Drakuliren/Shutterstock.com; pp. 4–5 (background) Outdoor_Media/Shutterstock.com; pp. 5, 6, 21, 47 Steve Oehlenschlager/Shutterstock.com; pp. 8, 17, 26, 34, 45 rck_953/Shutterstock .com; p. 9 tdixon8875/Shutterstock.com; pp. 10–11 © AP Images; p. 12 RubberBall Productions/Brand X Pictures/Getty Images; p. 15 FabrikaSimf/Shutterstock.com; p. 18 Nikolay Gyngazov/Shutterstock.com; pp. 22–23 Delmas Lehman/Shutterstock .com; p. 27 Kate Brady/Moment Select/Getty Images; p. 28 Nathan Krause/Shutterstock .com; p. 32 BW Folsom/Shutterstock.com; p. 35 Dennis Hallinan/Archive Photos /Getty Images; p. 37 dasytnik/Shutterstock.com; p. 41 Kirk Geisler/Shutterstock .com; pp. 42–43, 46 rodimov/Shutterstock.com; p. 50 robuart/Shutterstock.com.

Design: Michael Moy; Photo Research: Xina M. Uhl